Will Sam Make a Friend?

by Amy Houts
Illustrations by Laura Arias

Sam is new to the class.

"Come in, Sam," said Miss West.

Sam comes in.

"This is Sam," said Miss West.

"Hi, Sam," said the class.

Sam looks at the class.

Will she make a friend?

"This is Tom," said Miss West.

"Tom, help Sam with her bag."

"Put your bag in here," said Tom.

"Thanks," said Sam.

Sam smiles.

Will Tom be her friend?

It is time to sit.

"Will you sit by me?" said Tom.

"Yes," said Sam.

She smiles.

Tom is her new friend!